Jehovah Jukebox

Vice

Page 56

Jehovah Jukebox

Joan Jobe Smith

Event Horizon Press • 1993

Some of these poems originally appeared
in the following literary journals and publications:

The Wormwood Review
Inkshed (England)
Pearl
Purr
Scree
Nausea
Maelstrom Mini Review
River Rat Review
Mountain & High Plains Motorcycle Magazine
Poetic Space
Slipstream
Blow Up
408
Fred & Joan
One Page

Jehovah Jukebox

Copyright © 1993 Joan Jobe Smith. All Rights Reserved.

Library of Congress Catalog Card Number 93-70928.
ISBN 1-880391-07-4.

First Printing, September 1993.

Typography and Design by Joseph Cowles.

Cover art and drawing on page 64
adapted from French illustrations of the 1920s.
Frontispiece drawing by Joan Jobe Smith.

Back cover photograph of Joan Jobe Smith by Marilyn Johnson.

Published by:

Event Horizon Press
Post Office Box 867
Desert Hot Springs, California 92240

♾ Printed and Bound in the United States of America.

For the ones so nice to come home to—

Holly, Danny, Elaine

and Fred.

Foreword

I speak from the point of view of the somewhat old-fashioned American male: what we old guys love about Joan and her work is that she has known us at our worst, as, for instance, customers at go-go bars, and yet still manages not only to tolerate us but to find things about us to appreciate, even to desire. She might like us to clean up our acts a little, but she wouldn't want her world without us, and she doesn't want to sanitize us, let alone un-man us. That is also, by the way, one of the secrets of the success of the poetry magazine *Pearl,* of which Joan was the founding editor, and it explains why she and I can share an enthusiasm for the work of Charles Bukowski. She is liberated even from the shibboleths of liberation.

I like to think, however, that I would enjoy Joan's work even if she were the most notorious virago of our age—a title that would take some vying for. Ideology aside, I think I would still respond to the vividness of her memories, the authenticity of her reportage on a minutely observed world. She has the writer's eye, the writer's ear, the poet's delight in fresh and concise phrasing. If she weren't a friend, she would be a worthy foe. I don't think she would mind me characterizing her as the Wife of Bath with a brain. We have experienced the same decades from the differing yet overlapping perspectives of our genders. Often within the pages of the same periodicals—Marvin Malone's *Wormwood Review,* for instance—we tell two sides of the same (as ancient as it is postmodern) story.

GERALD LOCKLIN
California State University, Long Beach

"The world has shaped me and I

have shaped what I can."

—*Charles Bukowski*

Contents

... And The Ladies Of The Fred Astaire Fan Club

When Fred Astaire died, my girlfriend
Marlene sent me a sympathy card
in which she wrote, sincerely,
"May Mr. Astaire live in our hearts
forever," reminding me of our
Fred Astaire fan club of two
when we were go-go girls at
that divey Daisy Mae's
and had to dress like Daisy Mae
and dance to that off-key,
off-beat psychedelic band
with the LSD-corroded lead singer
who croaked when he did Hendrix
or Morrison. While my friend and I
bugalooed to "Purple Haze"
beneath the black lights
that made our teeth and polka dots glow
in the yellow haze of cigarette smoke,
we imagined we wore marabou,
danced the Continental with
Fred Astaire as he crooned
"Cheek to Cheek" so we didn't care
when a drunk reached to cop a feel.
Then, at 3 a.m., after we'd emptied
and scrubbed Daisy Mae's thousand ashtrays
and beer mugs, we'd rush home
to Fred Astaire and his top hat
on the late-late show chipper just
for us, just like Betty Grable
and her gams for the bombardiers,
Marianne and her valour
waiting in Marseilles for *les frères*,
something fine for us to come home to
after the war.

Stanley-Stella Things

When my husband took the money we'd saved
for the down payment on a tract home
to pay down on a go-go bar and started
working 24 hours a day, I wrote Dear Abby
and told her all about it, and how I thought
he was spending nights with a go-go girl.

A week after he left me for a go-go girl
who could do the Shimmy all night long,
Dear Abby wrote me back on stationery
that had her picture on it of her wearing
a dark brown hairdo ratted and combed into a flip
making her look like a go-go girl.
Trust him, she advised. Don't worry. Don't nag.
Though warm and wise, Dear Abby was still
in the early stage of her knowledge gathering,
a physician pre-penicillin yet to learn
the secrets of those important things
that happen between a man and woman in the dark,
Stanley-Stella things, Tennessee Williams warnings
people would come to know in the next decades.

I never wrote back to Dear Abby that she was wrong
or what happened, that I became a go-go girl
to support me and my kids,
began to wear my hair
in a ratted and combed flip
that I'd later let grow down to my waist
then whack off in grad school
in a fit of fear of stupidity,
perm it, now color it to hide the gray
as Dear Abby does today,
but I'll always feel
resting upon my shoulders
those dark brown flips,
angel wings in flight,
our tender, furry, little angel flips.

The Crotchwatchers

It took me a while to figure out
what the guys were looking at,
why they never looked at
our faces, and why Abner's 5
had built the bars so low down
that the guys couldn't, their noses
level with our knees, so that they
looked straight up when we bent down
to give them their beer.

In high school our faces
had been the most important things
and we worked hard putting Noxema,
Camay, and Cover Girl make-up on them
to make them look nice and clean.
But now Dee stuffed her bikini bottoms
with Kleenex to make her crotch
look bigger, Bev, Penny and Cheryl Lee
shaved theirs to make them nice and clean

and one day I figured it out
although I didn't want to
when a customer told me
you could tell all about a broad
from looking at her crotch,
how many kids she'd had,
how good she was in bed,
how many men she'd laid,
if she had the curse or the clap,
but,
ha-ha,
turn all you split-tails
upside-down,
ha-ha,
and all of you
look exactly alike.

Tits For Tat

Some of the guys likened us go-go girls
to the Golddiggers on Dean Martin's tv show,
the nouns "dingbat," "airhead," and "bimbo"
not yet a part of American feminine pejorative.

We were sequined and fringed jokes,
each month a new one about us in *Playboy* magazine,
and the guys would tell us,
"What do you call an old go-go girl?"
"I don't know."
"A went-went girl!"
and we were supposed to laugh and like it,
while they drank the beer we brought them
and ogled our tits and asses.

Their sixties' sexually repressed narrow-tied
and tight-panted minds
labeled a sexy woman a whore,
a woman who liked sex a nympho,
and a woman who wanted her own way
was either a ball-buster
or just like their bitchy mothers,
the pronunciation evolving daily
in front of our very ears to "muh-thuh,"
so we mined with fervor
the wantonness of their wallets,
dug the priapics of their pockets
for all the gold we could get
to pay for boob-jobs, new Mustangs, good dope,
and shoes and Disneyland
for our fatherless kids.

Symbiosis, it was, and they never realized the ecology.
We were the orchids thriving in the rot
of their tree trunks, cowbirds
picking ticks from their cowhides,
punch-lines, always, to their dirty jokes.
Tits and ass for tat.

One half of symbiosis is never very
pretty.

4

Easy Riders

On Sundays
the doldrums between
Saturday night's revelry-devilry
and Monday morning's misery of having
to start the whole week all over again
rain or shine
the bikers came into Abner's 5
not to see us go-go girls
but to take over
run off the pool hustlers
the surfers playing the Beach Boys on the jukebox
and the only ones not afraid
the World War 2 vets
and the serious boozers
drying out Saturday night's blackout on beer

and I wasn't as much afraid of the bikers
as I was their red eyes, snake and skull
tattoos, and their smells of sweat and grease
that would have warded off even the ancient evils
of a Cro-Magnon cave
because the bikers always called me Li'l' Darlin'
or Baby, and never pinched me
or tried to sell me dope

and now, years later, I like to think
like I did back then, that they respected me
being the psychics that they were with eyes
in the backs of their heads always on lookout
for the Law so they could make
laws of their own, and thought me
a cool chick even though
I was straight

but the truth was
I know now just like I really did then
that they didn't think I had the makings of
a good biker old lady

what with my scrawny bod
not sexy enough to tighten jeans
and perch upon the backs of their
big, black Harleys
like ripe, juicy melons
because they tossed me dollar tips
for each pitcher of beer I served them, their
quiet, diligent bribery
for me
another gnat on their highway
to stay the hell
out of their way.

A Groovy Kind Of Love

Crazy Ted,
a Registered Sexual Deviate
for homosexuality, a Navy and Nietzsche macho,
was a gentleman, my Don Quixote, and when
a biker or a pool hustler called me Twiggy,
he yelled at them as loud as he could,
"The meat's always sweeter next to the bone,"

and on slow days when I complained
I only made half the tips the other
sexier and bolder go-go girls did,
Crazy Ted always handed me a dollar,
put his hand on my shoulder, and told me
I was too good for All This,
and would someday marry a prince.

I would never marry a prince,
but on some Sunday afternoons,
Crazy Ted would fatten me up
on to-go steak and lobster dinners,
and some Sunday mornings,
when we were the only ones in Abner's 5,
he'd bring me Dom Perignon we'd sip
from a coffee mug, and Melba toast,
and Beluga caviar we'd spread,
for want of a knife, with the red handle
of my Maybelline mascara brush,

and Crazy Ted,
my Knight of the Crazy Countenance,
would hold up his mug of Dom Perignon,
look up at the windmills of broken
air conditioning in the ceiling,
smile as big as the moon does, and say,
quoting jukebox
rather than Cervantes,

We had a groovy kind of love.

Because I Could Spell Einstein

Crazy Ted, my only sugar daddy
at Abner's 5, was always trying to
kill himself, had as many suicide
scars on his wrists as a 40s' starlet.
Afterwards, after he'd drunk 10 or 20
Coors, and his big lips were loose
enough to sink ships, and his brown eyes
stormy enough to cry rivers, he'd always
want to talk to me About It. And I'd've
rather talked to my mother about my
shortcomings as a daughter, so I'd
pretend to be busy washing beer glasses,
emptying ashtrays, until Ted finally
passed out on the bar. I guessed It: the scars
had a lot to do with him getting kicked out
of the Navy for being a homosexual, then
being disowned by his well-to-do folks,
his working as an assembler
instead of as an aerospace
engineer, and being a drunk,
coming first to Abner's 5 after work
to dry out first on Coors
before going home to his pad next door
for his fifth-a-day Cutty Sark nightcap.
Ted had bent my ear just once,
and that was enough. Besides, I didn't
want to get any closer to a crazy man
than our mutual fingertips upon my tiptray,
although I guessed I'd miss his loony
grin if he ever really did himself in,
plus that dollar a day tip he left me
six days a week added up to a lot of
sugar a year for my kids' Rice Krispies.
Also, Ted always said he liked me
for my fine mind. I was the only
go-go girl he knew who could spell
Einstein.

"I" Before "E" Except After Einstein

Ted liked pear-shaped Pat, too,
because she had the guts to wear
a French-cut bikini with that
fat 50-inch butt of hers. He
liked Brandi Blue, too, because her
real name was Phyllis Fay. And
Sue because he could tell by the
way she walked that she'd once
studied ballet. Ted liked class,
bought us all Joy *parfum* for our
birthdays, had an alligator skin
wallet from Saks in which he had
his Registered Deviate I.D., the
goodbye-forever letter from his
well-to-do sister written on powder
blue Crane's watermarked bond.
Ted had class, too, at least a
little, because he could quote
Einstein, Nietzsche, and Nixon,
plus surpassed Kafka in absurdity, like
the day after one of his suicide
attempts, he came into Abner's 5
with the two ambulance drivers who'd
zoomed him to emergency, walked in
with his scrawny arms and white-
taped wrists wrapped around their
shoulders—a scarecrow Christ,
laughing his head off, happy to
have been saved from Good Friday.
"Bring my two good buddies a pitcher
on me," Ted said to me, and laughed,
and I did. "Spell Einstein for my
two good buddies," Ted said to me,
and I did, "i" before "e" except
after Einstein, and he laughed
until he cried, the tears streaming
down his cheeks as yellow as beer.
The ambulance drivers didn't laugh,
though. They'd never seen anything
like it in their lives.

S'Wonderful

It was payday, plus the first of the
month when Ted got his Navy pension
check, and he was laying dollar bills
on our tiptrays brick thick, making
us feel like Queen Bees, honeyed with
money, our go-go fringe feeling like
Broadway Baby marabou, so when he
asked us for the 100th time to go to
dinner at the Flite Rm across the
street to show us off to his buddies,
we chorused okay. Come shift change,
though, Pat went home to her old man
Ted didn't know about, Brandi Blue went
out with a good-looking pool hustler,
and Sue had an ulcer attack from all
that Cutty she'd sipped all day from
the fifth Ted had snuck in. I didn't
want to go alone, be showed off, be alone
with Crazy Ted to discuss the theory
of relativity for the 100th time, and I
was going to tell him so, but there he stood
at Abner's back door, all dolled-up in a wool
herringbone suit and vest in a heat wave, his
thick dark hair slicked back like a Dead-
End Kid, holding four white orchids, and
laughing Jack-in-the-box jolly until he, a
Flo Ziegfeld, saw that his Follies Girls
had dwindled to just me—Fanny Brice.
Ted thought for a moment, then grinned,
handed me the four white orchids, said,
"Two's company, my dear," and promenaded
me across the street where he ordered me
the Flight Rm's finest: *escargot*, Dom
Perignon, steak and lobster tail. Before
it arrived, though, Ted staggered into
the piano bar and stayed, drinking cognac
with his buddies, and requesting over and

over "S'Wonderful." Not being showed off,
not very hungry, I went home, where my ex-
old man sat smoking a cigar, waiting for me.
All night long he browbeat me, wanting to
know who my lover was. And all night long
I couldn't think up a good enough lie
to explain where I got those four white orchids,
because he refused to believe the truth.
The next day at Abner's 5, Ted and I
told the girls how "s'wonderful" dinner
had been, and from then on, Ted
always called me "my dear," and once in
a while, on payday, I'd let him kiss me
on the cheek.

The Gun On The Wall Next To His Heart

In my go-go novel, I killed off
Crazy Ted, had him blow out his own
brains with the gun he really did
carry next to his heart
in his Navy peacoat. One day Ted said he'd
get my ex-old man for me after he'd
heard he was harassing me. No, I
told him, and took him a Coors on me to
get him thinking about Nietzsche.
I didn't want to get busted for Murder
One, plus I didn't want to be
alone with Ted to discuss the gory
details. Feeling bad for killing
Ted off, sad I might have brought
him bad luck in real life, imitating
his life in my art, I tried to look
him up, see if he was all right, but
there was no Crazy Ted in the Long
Beach phone book, so I went to his
old apartment next door to the used-
to-be Abner's 5, now a dental clinic.
At 2-B, lace curtains hung in the window
where once Ted had nailed a gray
Navy blanket, and on the window sill
stood a rose in a bud vase instead of
a row of empty Coors cans. Once before,
I came to Ted's door, after a glass of
Gallo to get up nerve to ask him for money
to leave town, hide out from my ex-
old man who wouldn't leave me alone.
But when I saw Ted through a crack
in the Navy blanket, holding an empty
fifth of Cutty Sark, sitting in the dark
in a wooden chair, staring at the tv,
the tv tube-light hueing him Halloween-
dead, I left without knocking, just
like I did again, knowing that he

wasn't there. Passing the veterans'
hospital on the way home, I almost
stopped to see if he were in their
intensive care, being fed Cutty, i.v.

Ted would laugh till he cried a river
knowing how all those dollar bills he
gave me all those years had drawn
so much interest.

Purple Hearts

Smitty, the scared shitless Marine,
didn't want to go to war he told me
every Sunday afternoon after he drove
his junkheap 60 miles from El Toro
Marine Corps base to Abner's across the
street from the aircraft factory that
made the planes that dropped the bombs
on Vietnam and maybe Smitty some day.

Smitty's best buddy had already gone to Nam
and got blown apart by a land mine
Smitty told me every Sunday afternoon,
and then, drunk on blood, sweat, and Coors,
he'd play Bob Dylan on the jukebox,
"How does it feel to be on your own . . ."
over and over, lay his head on the bar
and weep until the pool hustlers shouted
"Hey, play something else goddammit!"

I might've said, There, there, to Smitty,
and bought him a beer, but he hated me
and the other go-go girls at Abner's 5,
calling us every Sunday dumb, lazy chicks
who didn't know what made the real world tick,
and I'd look around at my best buddies
who didn't know what made the real world tick:
Little Patti who worked double shifts
to support her four kids, Linda Lee who
gave all her tips to her old man Reuben
who beat her up whether he was stoned or down,
and Robin who ran away at 13 from a sadist stepdad
to earn a living in a stinky beer bar,
and not to mention what I was going through.
All of us spoils of the eternal war
between the sexes, the languishing war
fought in the darkest love forests and lust jungles.
Of course, we were the lucky soldiers who'd never
be blown apart by bombs or land mines, eaten to the

bone by Agent Orange, and we'd never have to
fear fear itself.

Too bad, though, that on those Sunday afternoons
I grew to hate Smitty, too. I'd liked to have
said, There, there, and a year later
when he came back from his tour of duty
welcomed him with open arms, bought him a beer.
But Smitty never came back to Abner's 5
like he said he would to tell us chicks
what was ticking and happening in the real world.
So I knew that Smitty'd either got blown apart
by a bomb or a land mine,
or fallen in love.

They All Said Arayna Was A Narc

They all said Arayna was a narc,
an alias if anyone ever heard of one,
a cop narc pig, they all said, because
girls who looked like her didn't work
in beer bars, not girls wearing silver
lamé and $400 hairpieces, one so long
it hung down to her butt, which was as
wide as a rococo whore's, and lazy as one,
always leaning against the bar or cash
register, while she re-pinned her hairpiece,
straightened her fishnet stockings, wiped the corners
of her pink lips glowing white under the
black lights. None of us ever saw her pour
a glass of beer or empty an ashtray, or even
light her own cigarette. The guys who came
in every day arm-wrestled for that pleasure
just to see her bend down, let it all—her
big, *baba au rum* breasts—hang out of her
bikini top into their faces. And all of them,
the execs in navy blue suits, the stevedores in
T-shirts, the bikers in greasy Levi's, all of
them handed her their money for no reason,
like bribery, ransom, her reward for being
so beautiful, and she'd put their money in a
beer pitcher that each night at quitting time
foamed over the brim with ten-dollar bills and
silver half-dollars. The day Arayna never came
back to work, we all told stories about what
happened to her, that she'd gotten knifed
in the parking lot by a Hell's Angels' jealous
old lady, shot by one of the night shift girls
after Arayna had finked on her, catching her
selling whites and pot, and that she'd finally
gone home one night with Big Red, the bouncer,
who said he was the best lay in town, had
mirrors on his ceiling over his bed, and she'd
refused to leave. Or the real story (maybe)

was that Arayna's husband, an aeronautical
engineer, had come in one day and saw her
dressed that way wearing nothing but silver
lamé, and dragged her out of the place
screaming, his hand clutching her real hair,
and drove her back to suburbia in his black Benz,
back home to her two dogs, one cat, a sick
goldfish, and three kids—and a kitchen full
of dirty dishes.

Ralph Bellamy

At the young age of 80, Delaney
still got horny, he told me.
Not wanting women his own age,
the dried up old bags, he placed
an ad in the *L.A. Free Press* that read
"Sweet young thing wanted. Free room
and board in exchange for PLEASURES."

He got one answer, but no photo.

He wrote her to meet him at Abner's 5
and he wore a suit and tie
(the same he wore to his wife's
funeral), but this time with a
white carnation in his lapel, so
she'd know which one he was sitting
on a barstool next to the jukebox,
just like he'd seen Ralph Bellamy do
when he waited at the Stork Club
for Irene Dunne.

Who never showed up either.

The Epidemiology Of The Permanent Breast

Brandi Blue wanted big breasts more than anything,
more than love, money, old age, or happiness,
her own breasts tiny pancakes she taped
to the top of her sequined padded push-up
a joke, a curse, a deformity,

so she was happy to pay a plastic surgeon
on Wilshire Boulevard $100 a week,
$50 per breast, to shoot into each
an ounce of silicone for 33 weeks
until she was a size 38D,

and as her chest
grew two perfect Mt. Everests,
I longed, too, to see
earth bountiful bounce beneath my chin,
so one day I went with Brandi Blue
to see her plastic surgeon,

saw Brandi Blue lie upon the examining table,
naked from the waist up beneath the sheet
as if she waited for a lover man
until finally the doctor entered
carrying a hypodermic syringe the size
of a bayonet he pushed into each breast, and
pulled out of each breast with such magnum force
that Brandi Blue wept until her ears filled with tears,
and I looked up to count the holes
in the acoustical ceiling
for many moments
while from each side of her breasts
a thin red ribbon of blood streamed down
like the drool of a
mammal-hungry, one-fanged vampire
in a very bad dream.

Frying Pork Chops Topless

Brandi Blue thought the topless craze
would cure us all—even The Establishment—
of our uptight ways and so after she got
silicone shots to size 38D she danced topless
for ten dollars an hour at the Purple Haze.

Brandi Blue wasn't a very good dancer
but she smiled and bumped and grinded
and the guys liked it, gave her
lots of tips, and one of the regulars,
a pool hustler, wanted to take her to bed.

Brandi Blue took him home with her
and cooked him his favorite food,
fried pork chops, topless, him grinning,
while the pork chop grease-pops flew
onto her jiggling breasts, making her
nipples good and hard.

I didn't approve of her frying pork chops
topless, especially in front of
her little girl, but Brandi Blue just
tweaked, don't be uptight,
be out of sight.

Brandi Blue married the pool hustler,
had his son, but the pool hustler
ran off with the baby sitter, and the
topless craze got mellow, the Purple Haze
only paying $5 an hour, so Brandi Blue
had to work stag parties, model for
soft porn, until her silicone went bad
and she had to have a mastectomy at age 31.

Brandi Blue became a reborn Christian,
had her name legally changed to Brandi Blue,
studied real estate, tried to learn to type,
went to nursing school and graduated.
Her daughter turned out to be weird and wild,

her son dyslexic, and now they rent rooms
in her tract home she bought with her
topless dancing money.

Brandi Blue had a hard life, all right,
but what bums me out the most was me not
approving of her frying pork chops topless.
It was the happiest time of her life.

To The Coy Mistresses

Delilah told me she'd show me
how to do Deep Throat and make a man
really happy, maybe win back my ex-old man,
but I told her I didn't want to do Deep Throat,
didn't want my ex-old man back
because he was too mean, and besides,
I wanted a man to make *me* really happy,
Deep Throat *me:* gently, but ecstatically
swallow and unswallow my earlobes,
my fingertips, and toes,

and Delilah got huffy with me,
said it was selfish women like me
who were responsible for the war
between the sexes, the sex hang-ups,
uptightness and taboos, and while she
rapped about Maypole wrapping,
the Zenishness of that peculiar
reverse peristalsis, Deep Throating,
I realized that it was unselfish women like her,
the flagrant fellatrices, dutifully delighted
by male genitalia, who were responsible
for the growth of men's cocks and balls to
the frogs smoking cigars they'd become
instead of the tadpoles they might've remained
in the hands and thimble throats of the
wronged women.

Jehovah Jukebox

The blue collar guys thought us
go-go girls were damned lucky
to work in a beerbar instead of
a hellhole like they did, we got
to do all the things they wanted to
do all day while they pushed and pulled
steel, we got to talk, smoke, shoot pool,
or drink a beer anytime we wanted to, plus
we got to listen to the jukebox all day long
for free.

Never mind that we'd never get vacation pay,
sick leave, overtime, or old age pensions,
that beer made us fat, the bar's darkness
and smoke making it another kind of hellhole,
and that the jukebox was as earbusting
and mindnumbing as their Jupiter machinery.

Never mind that instead of a crazy,
never-can-be-pleased supervisor
threatening lay-off, we had our own
nemesis reminder of our inferiority
and mortality: the Pastor Mick Jagger
fomenting foreboding every day
from the polycolored plastic jukebox pulpit
as he told us stupid girls, us honky-tonk
women under His thumb, having 19th nervous
breakdowns, the ways of the angry-handed
God-of-the-day, and screamed at us
that we couldn't get no satisfaction,
or what we want, and what a drag it was
getting oh-
old.

The 1992 L.A. Riots Bring Back Memories

The night of the Watts Riots
I went to work anyway at the Fort
the diviest, dirtiest beerbar ever
on the wrong side of the tracks
just 6 miles, as the crow flies, from Watts.

The doors of the Fort were locked
and after I knocked a long time
Mick my boss opened and said,
Fuck, man, what're you doing here?
You crazy or something, don't you
know there's a riot going on?
No, I didn't know about any riot,
I'd slept all day to work all night,
hadn't watched tv or read a newspaper,
my riotous world inhabited mostly by me,
my 3 kids and worries about overdue rent,
and then suddenly I realized that the
noises I'd heard on the freeway
on the way to work had been
sniper's rifles, not backfire.

Mick said, Come look,
leading me up to the roof
where the guys in the band
did drugs during their breaks
and he showed me the yellow fires
and red sky of Watts just 6 miles away.
The world is coming to a fucking end,
Mick said, not knowing then
that 1965 was merely Genesis 1
of what was to come and be.

Mick offered me a suck off his joint
and a quickie on the desk
in the storage room he called his office
but I said no and went on home
back down the deserted freeway
through the sniper fire, unafraid,

because I was only 25
and too busy staying alive
to realize yet that I was not immortal
and
that the world really could come to an end.

A Ticket To Ride

The Fort, built to look like one,
a go-go bar on the wrong side of the tracks,
and foghorn-listening distance from the L.A. Harbor
would not be the Moulin Rouge either.
Full of stevedores, merchant marines, sailors
and bikers, there would be no Manet or Toulouse
to sketch me while I stood pouring beer.
There would be no Jane Avril or *le cancan*,
only Carlita doing the Dog, the dirtiest dance
there'd ever be, on the stage in the middle
of the horseshoe bar close enough for the guys
to cop a feel while Carlita, on her hands
and knees, swinging her bikinied butt,
emulated perfectly a rutting dog.
There would be a drunken German sailor
who would twist my wrist thinking I stole
his dollar instead of taking it
to pay for the beer he ordered.
There would be the two 7-foot-tall Samoan bouncers
who would grab the drunken German sailor
by his shirt for twisting my wrist, hit him
on the head and shoulders with their sticks,
and throw him out the door onto the gravel
covered parking lot while he hollered
he'd get even with me for stealing his last dollar.

And when the rock-and-roll band came on
and beer prices doubled and the Chicano couples
came in to do the cha-cha, the stevedores,
merchant marines, sailors and bikers would leave
to go wherever to sleep it off to begin a new day
of meanness. And Carlita would scoop up enough
tips from them to fill a beer pitcher.

And until 2 in the morning I would think about
time and place, the chronological train
that takes some people to destinations
they do not choose.

At least the ticket to ride
was free.

Concert Bal Tous Les Soirs

Even I who'd only been
in the two beerbars I'd worked in so far
knew that the Fort was a hellhole,
knew that the Norwegian wharf rats the size of cats
who watched me in the storage room
used as a dressing room
were not Disneyesque, not to be
anthropomorphized,
that the 7-foot-tall Samoan brothers,
the bouncers, two dragons
wearing hornets' nest collars,
who smacked sawed-off pool sticks across their palms,
itchy for a fight, were not picturesque,
and Carlita and the other go-go girls
with teen-age-made gang tattoos
on their hands and rumps who stole my tips
when I wasn't looking,
were not black comedy,
but from the nether world of mirthlessness.

The Fort, a beer bottle's throw
away from the L.A. Harbor,
was the kind of dive you see in 40s' B movies
where the bad guys go to hire an assassin,
the kind of place where even Genghis
and his horde would've sat
with their backs against the walls,

and Crazy Ted,
a Navy vet of two Big Wars,
who'd received a Purple Heart,
who'd been knifed in dives from Pearl Harbor to Seoul,
and crazy to boot, knew that
the Fort was the worst dive of them all
because when he walked in
he rolled his eyes,
pulled up the collar of his Navy peacoat
to hide his clenching jaws,

and then, as he sipped his Coors, frowning,
as if it were poisoned, he told me
I'd better get the hell out of this place
before it was too late,
and while my back was turned dancing,
Crazy Ted snuck out,
even though he always carried a gun,

and that night I quit
but not because of the screws
that meant the obvious
some of the bikers left on my tiptrays,

and not because of the drunken German sailor
who was out to get me
because he thought I stole his dollar,

and not because of the carload of Mexicans
who waited for me down the street after work
and sang "La Bamba" while they
followed me to my freeway on-ramp,

or because of the gunshots I heard every night
coming from the railroad yard across the street,

or because of the lumps on the side of the road
I saw every night and was sure were corpses,

or because of the evaporating dream
of getting rich quick
working double shifts,

but because

I missed my kids.

Live: Miss Peggy Lee Singing
"Baubles, Bangles, And Beads"

Home at last,
away from the smoke and noise
of the coal mine, that beerbar,
I removed my beer-rotting shoes,
hairpiece and eyelashes, to bathe,
put on my nightgown,
then ate leftover supper
fixed by the lady I paid to watch my kids
six days a week

and while my kids slept
in my king-size bed sans husband
pressed together like puppies
waiting for me to come to bed and kiss them

and while the rest of the world spun past,
the Establishment,
the Weathermen,
the flower children,
the Manson murderers,
the Vietnam war,
the war protesters,
the student-shooting National Guards at Kent State,
the moon-walking astronauts,
the Black Panthers,
the Women's Liberation,
the Gay Liberation,
the Sexual Liberation,
the pot smokers, the acid-droppers, and vegetarians,

I lay on the sofa,
sipped a glass of milk,
listened to the hi-fi and LPs I bought in high school,
Sinatra, Mathis, Nat King Cole,
and dreamed about the other men I might've married
who surely would have saved me from all this,
oh, that Perfect Other Man, that wondrous god

from the twelfth of never,
who would have gotten me under his skin,
and in the wee small hours of the morning,
when he looked at the moon,
he would've
seen only me.
Unforgettable.
That's what we all are.

Dancing In The Dark

Now and then
when I wanted to clean up my go-go girl act,
get me a respectable job as a secretary
or clerk typist,
even though I'd earn two-thirds less money,
I'd get out my powder blue portable
Smith-Corona typewriter my parents gave me
when I graduated from high school
and my Learn-to-Type manual
I got at Long Beach City College
before I dropped out
and I'd put masking tape on the
typewriter keys and try to teach myself
to type a-s-d-f-g, h-j-k-l-semicolon
and q-w-e-r-t, y-u-i-o-p
until the tape came off
and my fingers stuck to the
masking tape glue on the keys,
so then I'd turn out the lights
so I couldn't cheat and look at the keyboard
and I'd try to type my mother a letter in the dark,
"Dwar Nithwr," I'd begin, "Gow arw tou/?"
and I'd keep on typing typos
my fingers getting stuck
unsticking the stuck keys in the dark
until my 8-year-old daughter
turned on the light and asked,
"Mommy, what are you doing
typing in the dark?"

And I answered,
just as she answered
when I caught her
with her hand in the cookie jar,

"Nothing."

On The Way To Disneyland

It will be an easy gig, baby,
said Richard, my agent, popping my
eardrums with the Juicy Fruit gum
he smacked into the telephone receiver.
Nothing like Whisky's, he promised,
where the go-go girl who was to follow me
didn't show up and Richard talked me
into dancing her gig, four hours straight
to the Rivington's pa-pa-pow-pow-pow, muh
maow-maow-maow-maow.
My blistered feet bled for days.
But I hated dance contests, I told him
especially phony ones,
sitting in a stinky bar half the night,
pretending to be an ordinary woman,
a secretary or something with my tarantula
false eyelashes and 4-foot long false hair,
waiting for the phony dance contest to begin
and I'd pretend to want to be in it,
jump up on the stage and undress
to my red-sequined bikini and do the
Jerk, the Pony, etc., each time losing
more respect for men who drank so much
they thought all women loved stripping
for strange men, and each time
respecting myself less for perpetuating
the myth, but the 50 bucks for
10 minutes of dancing would be
the most money I'd ever make in my life,

and the Shimmy Shack Tuesday Night Dance Contest
turned out even worse than I expected,
Richard booking Little Egypt who
danced in real leopard skins
with a real boa constrictor slithering
around her neck and pretending to be
an airline stewardess when the M.C. asked her,
and Suzie Q'd been booked, too, wearing her

silver lamé 4-inch spike heels to match her
G-string, Suzie Q now a stripper
at the Pussycat á Go-go off Sunset,
her pretending to be a former nun,
the drunk guys loving it and believing it
while Little Egypt and then Suzie Q
wiggled and writhed, bumped and grinded
to the guys' thunderous applause
and ooh's and ahh's, until too soon
it was my turn, and I groaned in the corner,
knowing I had miles to go-go, when suddenly,
a woman from out of the male maelstrom
yelled, "Me! Me! Me next!"
And up onto the stage jumped the most
ordinary 300-pound woman I'd ever seen,
wearing a big flowered muu-muu
and tasseled slipper sox, named Mary,
she told Nick the M.C. and Shimmy Shack owner,
dismayed as hell and glowering at Richard,
who shrugged and said,
She ain't one of my chicks,

and Mary told Nick she was a schoolteacher
from Oregon on vacation in Long Beach,
Califor-Nye-AY, and she loved to dance
to "Wooly Booly," so the band began to play,
and she yanked off her muu-muu,
but kept on her slipper sox, and revealed
that all she wore upon her pink,
freckled skin were a purple G-string
and purple tassels on two of the
biggest breasts I'd ever seen,
even in the dirtiest magazines,
and she could make one tasseled breast
go one way and the other the other way,
big purple propellers they were
on the fuselages of twin Spruce Gooses,

and the drunk guys, at least a hundred of them,
stomped their feet so hard that the
concrete floor and cinder block walls

of the Shimmy Shack vibrated
from the man-made earthquake,
and they hooted and whistled so hard
that Mary won, hands down, beyond a
shadow of a doubt, the Tuesday Night
Dance Contest, Mary the very first
Real Winner of the phony contest that
Nick and Richard had concocted, and Nick
actually had to pay a real $500 prize
to a real, ordinary woman, and afterwards
Nick and Richard had a big fight
in Nick's office, Nick calling Richard
an extortionist and swore never to hire
any more of his girls, but Nick was
nice to me, paid me the $50 anyway
for not doing anything, and the next day
I took my kids to Disneyland,
and bought them
everything they wanted.

What Pavlova Might've Done

No Pavlova, Isadora, or Ginger Rogers, me,
sometimes getting booed for not dancing sexy,
I hardly ever had any fans waiting for me
after my dancing jobs to get a closer look,
so when I saw the two Mexican guys
standing next to my car in the parking lot
of Joe's Bar & Grill in the middle of nowhere
in Pomona County, I thought they were
just hanging around, until I got up close
and one of them clicked open a switchblade
and called me *"Puta!"*
Then I recognized them, the two whose beers
I'd kicked over inside Joe's when they
sat too close to the stage. When they
complained to Joe and demanded more beer
on the house, he called them wetbacks
and kicked them out. Strong from dancing,
I could have outrun them but my high-heels
were stuck in the August-hot ooze of the
parking lot asphalt. And I couldn't yell
for help because there was no one for miles
except for Joe inside where the jukebox
blared full blast. The Mexican wiggled the
switchblade in the air like a pet snake and
said he was going to cut my tires and then me
even though he looked as scared and nervous
as I was, so using my slowest, 1-year-of-high-school
present tense Spanish I explained that I was
no whore, just a dancer, had kids, but no *esposo.*
Then I offered them the $30 Joe'd paid me
for 3 hours and suddenly, thanks to the money
plus the high-noon August sun,
they turned thirsty instead of murderous,
grabbed the money and ran off, disappearing
into the tumbleweeds and erewhon of heat and dust.

I drove to the nearest police station
to tell them what happened but they told me

it was just hearsay and they couldn't do anything,
and besides, a broad going around looking like me
in broad daylight wearing her hair like that
and a mini-skirt was asking for trouble,
so I drove on home
wondering what
Pavlova might've done.

Pretty Pauline At The Piano Bar

None of the old guys at the Lamplighter Inn
wanted me there go-go dancing on the just-
built stage covering the hole left in the
corner when they removed Pretty Pauline's piano.
The old guys hated this go-go thing,
the Soul music, the Doors, and the Stones,
so they sabotaged by playing "Moon River,"
Sinatra, or swing on the jukebox, none of
them noticing or caring when I danced a fox trot
or jitterbug to please them, determined
to keep hating me, staying faithful to their
Pretty Pauline no longer at the piano bar
whose pretty photo was still pasted
on the wall behind me, me wearing fringed
bikini, her wearing a white Doris Day
hairdo and smile and a black cocktail dress
showing just an inch of cleavage.

I didn't blame the old guys for liking her best,
and I admired their old soldier loyalty
to a finer, more ladylike cause. I would've
much preferred to sit with them at the bar
drinking scotch and requesting Pretty Pauline
to play "Stardust," then booing and hissing
with them the things that would soon replace me:
the topless dancer, the bottomless dancer,
disco, jock bars, and female mud wrestlers.
None of that or anything ever would ever be
as pretty as Pretty Pauline at the Piano Bar
playing "Stardust" sweeter than old
Hoagie Himself Carmichael
ever did.

Otis Redding

How I loved that man's music,
loved to dance to his "Shake,"
"Satisfaction," and "Dock of the Bay,"
his voice a satin wind of soul-man rhythms
cool and fine upon my sweaty bod
and hot, rocked-out high-heel shoes.

The night he died
at breakfast after work
all of us go-go girls and our boyfriends
talked about what would happen
to soul music now that Otis
was no longer around until Bobbie Jeen
who was from Mississippi said, "Hell,
he was just another nigger,"
and my eyes filled with tears
but I tried to hide it to be
far out and groovy
until my eyelashes fell off
so I went on home
where I felt useless and colorless
until the sun came up.

Months later, after Martin Luther King
got blown away, and RFK got blown away
(as Bobbie Jeen, the pool hustlers
and the dopers called it),
I was still dancing to Otis Redding every night
who still lived every night on the jukebox,
me doing the Temptation Walk and the Shing-a-ling
to "Dock of the Bay"
and realizing,
keeping my false eyelashes dry,
that Otis was letting us know
in those sweet, good songs of his
among those sour, bad times
that from then on
the blues would belong
to everyone.

California Dreamin'

Mary Kay left her home state
where they grew corn the color of her hair
and wheat the color of her skin
to come to L.A. in her VW to go-go dance on tv
and get rich, maybe marry Bobby Sherman
or one of the Righteous Brothers, but on the way
she turned off the wrong freeway off-ramp
and landed at Daisy Mae's. But it was okay,
Mary Kay dug wearing the red polka-dotted top
and black bikini bottoms and how the customers
ogled and copped feels while she wiggled
an innocent stripper-type little prance on the stage,
pelvic-thrusting in front of Bearded Ben's face
who leaned every night against the jukebox
selling pot, acid, and uppers, although
Marlene and I warned her that he wâs a
heartbreaker, a Midnight Rambler, The Rapper,
who got it on with all the new Daisy Mae girls
and dropped them after a couple months.
Oh, no, said Mary Kay, dreamily high on Oaxaca,
this is different. We're in love.
This Midwest farmer's daughter, not doing
what she ought to, was having fun
raising dope hell in the California sun,
being a California girl getting a suntan
and blonder and thinner from not eating anything
but pills, organic mesc, and Bearded Ben.
And sure enough, soon he started selling his stuff
from the jukebox at the Blue Bunny to hustle chicks
there like he always did when he was sick
of a Daisy Mae girl, and Mary Kay stopped smiling,
dancing sexy, coming down from dope, not getting it
for free anymore, and she began to cry a lot,
thinking about the man that got away, and when the band
played slow songs she'd tell Marlene and me
how big the stars and sunflowers were back home,
how there wasn't any smog, until one night

while she danced to "Crimson and clover,
over and over, over and over . . . " and people
tripped out, worked it on out in their purple ways
in the Daisy Mae yellow haze of cigarette smoke
to the off-keyed, LSD-corroded vocalist,
Mary Kay cracked up on stage, kicked
5 pitchers of beer onto the floor, screamed, then split
out Daisy Mae's front door to go back home in her VW
to the corn and wheat, stars and sunflowers,
wearing nothing but her polka dots and black bikini
and white sunstreaked hair the color of beer foam
and suntan the blotchy shade of brown
of a barroom floor.

Fallen Saint At The Wrong River

Dirty Dave the Daisy Mae manager
wouldn't throw the drunk guy out
even though he was asleep on the bar
which was against ABC regulations,
his greasy head balanced on the rim of his
beer glass, a fallen saint at the wrong river,
and when I tried to move his glass out from under
his head so he wouldn't tip it over and get cut
if he woke up, he woke up, grabbed my wrist,
called me a stupid barmaid,
and said to leave his beer the hell alone.

After the drunk guy unzipped his pants
and pulled out his penis for me to see,
Dirty Dave still wouldn't throw him out,
because he was too busy leaning on the jukebox
and talking to Bearded Ben
who'd just scored some good Colombian hashish,
and besides, Dirty Dave said, since nobody else
but me could see his dick, why hassle the guy.

When the drunk guy urinated on the floor
Dirty Dave still wouldn't throw him out,
just motioned for the gofer to mop it up
then me to move the mop handle and bucket
out of the aisle where customers walked
while he handed Bearded Ben a wad of money.

When the drunk guy turned around
to show everyone sitting at the tables—
men, women, and Dirty Dave alike
his erection he held in his hand
Dirty Dave shook Bearded Ben's hand
in gentlemanly dope-dealing agreement,
set his Coke on the jukebox,
walked over to the drunk guy
and with one hand yanked him off the barstool,
carried him through the bar

like a sack of rotten lunch,
threw him against Daisy Mae's door
that opened from the force,
spitting him outside.

On his way back to the jukebox to lean some more
Dirty Dave said to me,
his eyes a black stripe across
his Edward G. Robinson face,
"Goddamn I hate Mexicans."

Go-Go Girl Reunion

Those who don't show up at reunions
either have something to hide
or think they're too good. So
since go-go girls once let it all hang out
of bikinis and can claim neither that vice
nor virtue, we all showed up at the
Playgal Club where 10 years before we'd
all slung beer and shook our tail feathers
till 2 a.m. Karen, the most beautiful
and best dancer, was there wearing Shantung
and Joy *parfum*, the only one of us
to marry a millionaire
although we all tried. Brandi Blue was there
now thinner and a reborn Christian;
Suzie Q, too, in spite of warrants
out for her arrest. Judy was still
a barmaid, but now lived with a
younger, better-looking, better-
shooting pool hustler. Cheryl Lee
just got a new Z, a nose job, a
boob job and an abortion, too, all
paid for by one of her old sugar
daddies who wasn't the daddy. And
Deena, wearing thick glasses, her
eyes having gone bad from taking
too much LSD, had gone straight,
and now drank nothing but Southern
Comfort on the rocks. Betty had
given up macramé and now taught
aerobics; Katie got her real estate
license and a perm; Barbi got her
Ph.D. in psychology but said she'd
seen more weirdos when she worked
at the Playgal than she ever had
in a psycho ward. The new Playgal
owner, Dick Dale, had the band play
"Night Train" and all the old go-go

girls drunk enough got up on the stage,
raised their skirts up over their knees
and wiggled around. Dick Dale took
Polaroids and said over the microphone
to the audience and to us that we
weren't getting older, we were only
getting better, and over the whistles
and applause, I heard one of his 20 something
waitresses laugh and say to a cohort,
"Yeah, sure," knowing that she would
never show up to any reunion of any kind.
Wizened with young, she thought she knew how
to hold back sunsets with her tongue.

You, With The Stars In Your Eyes

At the Playgal Club, us go-go girls
didn't have a dressing room and had to use
the Ladies Room each night to pin on our
sequins and fringe and hairpieces
and take our 5-minute smoke-and-pee breaks,
Spike, our Simon Legree boss timing us, with a
stopwatch, and if we stayed longer than 6 minutes
he kicked on the Ladies Room door, yelled inside,
ironically rhyming, "Hey! Get your ass down the ramp,
you little tramp!"

During our first break, the guys' wives and dates
frowned at our tarantula eyelashes,
scorned our French bikinis still outlawed
on California state beaches, letting us know
that they were the real ladies in the Ladies Room,
sometimes one of them asking,
"How can you *do* such a thing?"
But then, during our second break,
after they'd had a few beers, they'd ask
what kind of eyelash glue or hairspray we used,
how did we learn to do the Pony, Jerk,
and Mashed Potato so good, and sometimes say,
"You're so lucky to work here."

Oh yeah, oh sure, we'd say, cynic hearts beating
beneath the push-up bras, our feet and hamstrings
aching, our hair and bikinis reeking
of beer, smoke and sweat, but yet,
deep down inside, just for a moment,
we were flattered into feeling like a movie star,
a homecoming queen, Gracie Slick, or Cher,
these drunken, blurry-eyed women
who led ordinary lives as housewives and secretaries
giving us the only sincere compliment of the night,
or week, until Spike kicked open the Ladies Room door again
and yelled inside,
"Hey!"

Noble Savages

Every night
after the Playgal Club closed
and us go-go girls had scrubbed all the
tables and chairs and barstools and
washed all the glasses and pitchers and ashtrays
and the beer mold from the backbar rubber mats,
scrubbed the mirrors, and soaked the bar towels
in bleach for the dayshift girls to rinse and fold,
all us go-go girls sat behind the bar
to smoke our third cigarette of the night
to listen to Spike, the manager, who stood by
the cash register to tell us how shitty we all were:
we weren't pretty enough
we didn't dance good enough
we didn't smile enough
we didn't hustle enough beer
because Saturday night's cash register receipts
were down again from last Saturday night's
and it was all because Spike saw Deena
jaw-jag 20 minutes with some pool hustlers,
Sherry took a 10-minute piss break,
Judy G. took puffs off a customer's cigarette all night,
Linda Lee ate a Hershey bar behind the bar,
Brandi Blue danced barefoot to "Night Train," and I
got to the stage two minutes late for "Wooly Booly."
Tomorrow night, Spike said every Saturday night,
one of us girls who didn't do her job right
was going to get fired to set an example
to the others who might want to start fucking off, too.
And Spike meant it, he fired a girl every Sunday night,
because this club was going to MAKE MONEY. SELL BEER.

The owner of the Playgal Club already
owned a Newport Beach bayfront pad and a yacht.
Soon he'd become a millionaire, thanks to luck,
his insight to making a buck, and our tits and asses,
fast beer-slinging and shaking of tail feathers.

But, yet, us go-go girls had to admit,
later while we put on our mini-skirts
in the Ladies Room, Spike and the Playgal Club owner
didn't treat us go-go girls half as bad
as Andrew Jackson did the
Cherokees.

When It Was Fun, It Was Very Very Fun

Sometimes it was fun being a go-go girl,
usually on payday, and probably
when it was a full moon, some nights when
everyone was inexplicably happy, even Spike, the boss,
because the place was packed and he was tripping
on some good acid, and Rick the machinist
was happy, had brought us girls a 5-pound
Whitman's Sampler and made us new tiptrays
on his machine, carved our names on them,
then painted them fluorescent to glow under
the black lights, our names in lights at last.
And Big Dave and Little Jim were happy,
having brought their camera to take our pictures
when Spike wasn't looking, and Dick Dale's
surfer guitar was hanging ten, so hot
that the guys and their dates now and then got up
to do the Twist and the bouncers didn't make them
sit down, and the pool hustlers were winning
and tipping for the first time in months. Even
Fat Bob was tipping two dimes instead of just one,
and Suzie Q was getting married instead of
getting an abortion, and two celebrities
wanted to date us, and the three tables of El Toro
Marines were *back* from Nam, and a customer
who was cute gave Cheryl Lee a real pearl ring,
and after I danced football signals—off-sides,
time out, touchdown—to "Mony Mony," my favorite
customer who only came in every six months gave me
$5 and told me again that I was as funny as
Carole Lombard and how for sure soon I would
get discovered, and afterwards, all of us out
for breakfast, we were all still happy,
and I could afford steak and eggs
and a slice of fresh strawberry pie.

And later in bed before sunrise
I'd think how fun it had been, how
someday I'd look back on all this and think . . .

but then, tomorrow
was another day.

I Never Went To Bed With The Famous Astronaut

Although the famous astronaut
clichéd what's a nice girl like
you doing in a dump like this, I
knew he thought me a tramp just like
all the other go-go girls he'd met
in all the beer joints he'd been in.
He told me the dirtiest jokes I'd
ever heard and kept yanking me down
to whisper secrets in my ear and
sometimes stuck in his tongue so far
I could feel it on my retina.
He said he'd give It to me any way
I wanted, but all I wanted was his
autograph. I had other things on
my mind, like my overdue rent and
my ex-husband who was harassing me.
So the famous astronaut told me
he'd tell me what it was like in
outer space if I had dinner with him
and drinks later in his hotel room.
I didn't show up, and the next day,
while I was on the stage dancing
to Lovin' Spoonful, he came in,
stood with his hands on his hips,
glowered at me and said, just
who in the hell do you think you
are, you little tramp, and then he
left, slamming the sunshine and door
behind him. The famous astronaut
had the right stuff, all right, he'd
met the President of the United States,
seen earth from outer space where
he'd defied gravity and nausea for
Americans like myself. He even
had a nice smile. But I had
my mean ex-old man and
overdue rent on my mind.

Heet

I still have the Heet in my medicine
cabinet, kept it for years, at first
in case I ever had to go back to dancing
and needed it, and then I kept it
because the orange box looked funky,
the analgesic and applicator inside
the bottle a vestige of go-go pain
of yore, those fossils of twisted
ligaments, bugalooed bones, so sore
some nights after 8 hours in the land
of 1,000 dances doing the Pony and the
Mashed Potato I'd have to lift my own
legs into my VW to drive home, then
crawl like a dog up the stairs to my bed.

The guys watching us all night at the
Playgal Club wouldn't have wanted to know
such pathos, our unglamourous after-hours,
the piss-like beer stains on our white fringe,
our rotting shoes from the salt poured
on the bar floors so we wouldn't slip
in the beer sludge, or the cigarette ashes
like coal dust under our white fingernails
that glowed opal under blacklights where
everything was always clean and bright.

Lucky that the Playgal Simon Legree
owner wouldn't let us talk much
to the guys, made us keep on dancin'
and a-prancin', shaking tail feathers,
smiling, and slinging pitchers of beer,
because had we been able to speak
like the courtesans the guys imagined us
to be, we would've told about the
cracks in the Versailles mirrors,
the holes in the bows of the ships
harbored in Marseilles, and then
all of us girls would have lost our heads
to the guillotine, and the guys lost at sea,
hung over, without a drop of Coors to drink.
And no longer horny.

Direct Object Of The Subjective Case

The old guys, and some of the young guys,
too, always wanted to buy a piece of our go-go
fringe or a sequin, something to
remember us by, they said, sometimes
even wanting to buy for twice what we
paid, our dancing tights, unwashed,
and once this old guy at the Shimmy Shack
wanted to buy my towel I used to wipe
my breasts and forehead and back
between songs, hot from the yellow
spotlights, and no air conditioning.
A dollar, he offered, and I said no,
knowing, no longer a Catholic, a go-go
dancer going on 5 years, exactly what
he wanted the towel for. Two, he said,
tossing another bill on my tiptray,
and I said no, and danced to the Stones'
"Satisfaction." Five he said, and tossed,
and I ignored him and danced to Wilson
Pickett's "In The Midnight Hour."
Six, seven, eight, he said, just for a
keepsake, baby, something for me to
wish on. But I'd read Havelock Ellis
and Freud and said no.
Even when he put a fifty-dollar-bill
on my tiptray I said no, and finally
he got up to go, scooped up his money
and said, Hell, a skinny-assed dame
like you ain't worth fifty bucks!
Then he staggered away just as the
two navy-blue suited aerospace execs
who'd been talking shop in front of me
suddenly took an interest in me,
taking me for a lady of the night and
ill-repute instead of a poor working girl,
and eyeing up my fringe and sequins, they
began tossing money on my tiptray,

and while I danced to that long, long
version of the Doors' "Light My Fire,"
I had fantastic fetishes of my own,
my libidinous dream of someday
going back to college, becoming an
English teacher wearing alligator pumps
and flower print dresses and teaching,
sincerely and patiently,
the direct object of the subjective case.

Dancing In The Frying Pan

He waited for me in the Blue Bunny parking lot,
the only guy out of the 100 who'd watched me dance
who thought me cute enough to wait for,
amazing me, especially since the dancer
before me was a six-foot tall Vegas showgirl
and the one after me was a purple-fringed
flurry who danced like Tina Turner.

He wore an expensive suit, had blow-dried hair,
drove a black Jag, handed me one red rose
laced with baby's breath, and told me
he wanted to show me a good time, prime rib
at Lawry's, jazz at The Lighthouse, he even
had a Playboy Club Key. He'd do anything
for me, he told me, and he meant *anything*.

For a moment I thought he might be Mr. Right.
The One who'd take me away from all this,
pay my kids' college tuition, mow my lawn,
but while I imagined our Hawaii honeymoon,
his wedding ring glittered in the sunset,
and a shadow cast across the bulge beneath
the zipper of his tight trousers—his anything.
"Sorry, dude," I put on, starting up my car.
"But I ain't got no time. I got to pose nude,
then I'm doin' a *ménage à trois*."

Turned on, hearing the things he expected
from the little tramp he perceived me to be,
he smiled big, handed me his business card,
told me to call him, anytime, day or night,
and I said yeah, sure, and drove away, knowing
that Monday morning he'd tell his fellow execs
about the potential Strange Stuff he'd met
the other night, and they'd laugh, my lies
much funnier than the truth, that I
was going home to my kids to take them to
Bob's Big Boy and then to see "Chitty-Chitty Bang Bang,"

after, though, they'd rubbed my knees and feet
and walked on my back and thighs with their bare feet
because my muscles were so sore
and I was so goddamned sick and tired of
dancing.

A Vaudeville Of Devils

For months I'd managed to keep it
secret from my landlord that my
husband had left me and I was working
as a go-go girl

for my landlord hated divorcées,
called them whores and broke their
windows and porchlights
to get them to move out,
he was the kind of man
who would've enjoyed piling stones
upon witches' breasts until they confessed
fellatio with Satan,
but mostly he was the kind of man
who becomes a landlord
because he loved being called a lord,

and because it was his land,
his God's little acre of 2-bedroom apartments,
after he found out about me being a go-go girl,
he broke my windows and porchlight
just as I expected,
glass everywhere, even in my bowl of Cheerios,
my kids scared, my baby screaming,
the neighbors wondering, while I loaded up
furniture, dishes, clothes and toys in a hurry
onto a trailer why he called me whore

which I really didn't mind so much
for I understood his urge to purge his soul
with rants, I knew his kind of man by then
who saw women only as rectangular empty boxes
meant to be filled with things of men,
for by then I'd become all women of the without,
a whore, a witch, and a go-go girl
dancing in a vaudeville
of devils.

Vice

Even though in L.A. strippers
and topless dancers bumped and grinded,
they began to arrest the go-go girls
in Long Beach, the city leaders
deciding that go-go girls doing
the Twist, the Monkey, the
Mashed Potato, and the Funky
Chicken were lewd and obscene.

So plainclothes vice officers sat in the bars
day and night drinking beer and waiting for us
to dance and then they'd flash their badges,
help us off the stage, and slap handcuffs
on us while the jukebox played on without us.

Those plainclothes cops must've gotten a kick
out of driving us ratted-haired, tarantula-eye-
lashed sequined girls down Long Beach streets
to the police department, stopping at the
lights while upstanding citizens stared
at the captured passengers in the
back seat of the plainclothes cop car.

The girls got a kick out of it,
the cop whistles while they were booked,
mug-shot, and bailed out. They always
came back to work and bragged about
their police record for doing the Twist,
the Monkey, the Mashed Potato, the Pony
and the Funky Chicken, alleged obscenities
that decades later would sound silly,
like the names of childrens' games.

I was too young and a little stupid
to realize the absurdity of it all,
the yin and yang of cosmic idiocy,
but soon I would read the poet Charles Bukowski

who wrote about those go-go girls getting
arrested, summing up that he guessed that
those Supreme Court boys
couldn't get it up anymore,

and suddenly it would all make sense:
that Time always marches on
without making one bit of sense at the time.

Right As Rain

When my father found out
about me being a go-go dancer
he turned red as sunburn
and nearly died young then
instead of a year later.
A juke joint dive! he yelled
when I got home, him
and my mother coming down to
Long Beach from Sacramento
surprising me, catching me
in the worst act of my life.
It's a nice place I explained.
A honky-tonk hellhole! he yelled,
his Texas drawl as baritonal
as tornado, him grinding his teeth
and chain-smoking Lucky Strikes.
The guys are nice, I explained,
aerospace execs, Vietnam marines,
Cal State grad students,
sometimes astronauts.
Drunkards! he yelled.
But I'm a go-go girl, I bragged.
You're a fringed floozie! he yelled,
the prodigal jazz dancer's pedant papa
a *vox savant* of morality, a Newton
holding a wormy apple, a van
Leeuwenhock eyeing grandiose beasties,
so I didn't explain that I did it
because I made more money in one week
than he did in three.
I'd soon quit dancing for other reasons,
but right then he was right as rain because
he was my father.

No Sweat

One day when I'd had it
with the go-go world
I went to find my mean ex-old man
to ask him to pay me child support
so I could quit, go back to school, learn to type,
and find a respectable job

and I found him at a beauty college on Pine St.
where he'd just started to be a hairdresser,
an odd thing I thought for a mean man like him
to want to be until it dawned on me
it'd be a good place for him to meet chicks

and we stood out on the sidewalk, him clicking
his haircutting scissors at me,
me squinting up at him and the cigar
he rolled like a log over big, Goliath teeth,
me telling him I needed child support
and finally him saying,
No way you'll ever get a dime out of me

and I never did, not even for my X-rays,
landlord and doctor after he,
being his meanest ever,
smashed up my face and apartment,
both of us in a crazy place of our lives
trying to find a way
in the days of up, up and away California dreamin'
to make a living with no sweat

but instead he'd go to prison
and just get meaner
and I'd waste time for many years
remembering the feel of his soft scrotum
in my palm just before I yanked,
trying to save myself,
him trying to yank the electricity from my throat
as I yelled for help
from somebody

just any old body.

Intimacy

Painting my face,
dressing, undressing in shocking pink,
passionate purple, or whorehouse red
velvet wallpapered go-go bar dressing rooms,
I saw enough smooth-skinned,
pink- or bruised-skinned, or
stretch-marked, pear-, cantaloupe-,
or fried-eggs-on-a-nail-shaped
tits and asses to satisfy a Peeping Tom's
curiosity of the female anatomy
for at least nine lives
and I listened to between-you-and-me-
and-the-lamppost go-go girl talk
like the size of Big Red's cock
that Robin and blonde-haired Penny shared
when they were between boyfriends,
what heroin cold turkey and jail were like
when they caught you for forgery,
what Linda Lee's stepfather did
while her mother slept,
the embroidery of face-wire after
your mean old man breaks your jaw,
and that Brandi Blue's real name
was Phyllis Fay.
We were Delilah, Salome, Jane Avril,
and Gypsy Rose Lee. We knew
what happened to Samson's hair,
the Baptist's head, why Toulouse longed
for absinthe, and who was the real father
of the child in our wombs. We knew
the original loony tunes, and go-go steps
danced in the Cro-Magnon caves by moonlight
and when my 8-year-old daughter
wanted me to join the PTA, have
coffee and cake with the other mothers,
I could not explain why I could not, or
my face paint extraordinaire
with which I was stained.

Boredome

Boredome, not *ennui*, I called my boredom
en faux francaise,
bored from dancing all day
or all night, the guys bored too now
with this going-over-the-hill go-go thing
a big, still-kicking, dying horse
and while the guys weren't watching,
while they talked shop, Nam, sports, and tv
or watched another, prettier, go-go girl
I did my own thing to those
jukebox songs impossible to dance to,

danced to the Righteous Brothers' "Ebb Tide"
my Twyla Tharp moderne, pirouetted
and pressed my fists to my forehead and heart,

danced to the Stones' "Sympathy For The Devil"
my Josephine Baker banana dance,
rolled my eyes, scratched imaginary
monkey fleas from my ribs and armpits,

danced to the Doors' long-long "Light My Fire"
my Cleopatran asp dance,
and to the Beatles' "Ob La De Ob La Da"
I danced a yo-ho-ho hornpipe,

one guy watching, though,
my boss,
the mean one with the
Edward G. Robinson eyebrows
warning me one more time
to clean up my act before he fired my ass,
patting my red-sequined ass
while he stared into smoky, blacklighted space,
wondering what he'd do for a living
after they closed down this place.

You Should've Seen This Place A Year Ago

Nobody came to see Ike and Tina anymore,
or stand in line an hour to hear the Platters
sing golden oldies, nobody came to drop acid
and sip Coke and trip out on the strobe lights,
psychedelic band, and the go-go girls' white
fringe and teeth glowing in the dark anymore.
Janis, Jimi, and the Doors were dead and nobody
wanted to pay as much for a pitcher of beer
as a Big Mac, fries, and a malt cost anymore,
or wanted to wear patchouli and patched jeans,
live on a commune in Oregon, or hitchhike 101
with a harmonica and a gallon of Gallo.

Everybody listened to Rod McKuen instead of Dylan,
they didn't have Nixon to kick around anymore,
nobody cared about Alan Watts, Leary, or the MIAs.
Women stopped burning their bras, began to
cut and blow-dry their hair, want babies,
and to wear pretty dresses.

It was over, and we knew it was over even before
Bearded Ben, out of jail and on probation,
shaved and started studying real estate, we
knew it was over even before the astronauts
told us that the moon was not brie, and Dirty
Dave painted his VW bus covered with zodiac signs
white and laid off us go-go girls and told us
to go to work in offices, coffee shops, or go on
welfare or to college and get student loans.

We knew even before 12-year-old girls began to
wear string bikinis on state beaches and *Playboy*
magazine showed pubes that it was over, that soon
Abner's 5 would become a dental clinic,
the Playgal Club a video rental store,
and Daisy Mae's bulldozed so's to build
a 7-story bank building surrounded by BMWs,
eucalyptus trees, and night-blooming jasmine.

Even in the beginning when the smiling men
threw dollar bills at us like pennies at a
wishing well, when our hair was real,
our black stockings clean, our new Mustangs
shiny, we knew that no thing, no place
ever stays the same until it's the same again,
and even then we wondered:

What's next?

Joan Jobe Smith received her Master of Fine Arts from the University of California, Irvine. The founding editor of *Pearl*, she lives in Long Beach, California.

Publisher's Note:

We ask our authors to complete a questionnaire which, among many other things, asks "Why is the book important?" and "How will it benefit its readers?" Joan's delightful reply is worth passing along to the readers of *Jehovah Jukebox*:

"Except for Rachel Carson's *Silent Spring* or *Webster's Collegiate*, is any book really important?

"Well, surely for the author it is, so of course I shall write that my book is *muy importante* in that it documents a peculiarly significant decade of social and sexual behavior, a transitional time when women were burning their bras and men taking off their ties to wear tie-dyes.

"Getting it on, socking it to ya, letting it all hang out were the '60s hip patois to live by while everyone liberated themselves from '50s repression (uptightness) to make way for and create the party-down times of the '70s, then the time-to-pay-the-fiddler days of the '80s.

"Benefit to the readers? Hopefully entertainment, vicarious pleasure of Being There and seeing how the other half, or the beginning half of a counter-culture lived. Hopefully insight and enlightenment, too, to some of the early vestige-suffering of the Single Mother, an anomaly then in the '60s, and now the mainstay of society."

It is with great pleasure that Event Horizon Press presents this collection of Joan Jobe Smith's poems, "written by a go-go girl of yore about the yellow haze and purple ways of life in a land of a thousand dances."

Poetry from Event Horizon Press

Cafes of Childhood
R. Nikolas Macioci, 1992

Confetti
Barbara Hauk, 1993

Deep Red
Donna Hilbert, 1993

The Firebird Poems
Gerald Locklin, 1992

Goodstone
Fred Voss, 1991

Mansions
Donna Hilbert, 1990

A Necessary Fire
Marilyn Johnson, 1992

Rodeo and the Mimosa Tree
Jennifer Olds, 1991

Voices From The Ho Chi Minh Trail
Larry Rottmann, 1993

For a catalog of all our titles, please write:

Event Horizon Press
Post Office Box 867
Desert Hot Springs, California 92240